JUSTICE

THE MINERS' STRIKE 1984-85

COVER: from a
photograph taken at
Bilston Glen Colliery,
Midlothian, Scotland,
by Val Wilmer/Format

Campaign Group
of Labour MPs

JUSTICE

THE MINERS STRIKE 1984-85

DENNIS SKINNER MP
TONY BENN MP
BOB CLAY MP
JOY COPLEY
BILL ETHERINGTON
MARINA LEWYCKA
ALAN MEALE
PAUL STANLEY
ROGER WINDSOR

VERSO

Whilst the contents of this pamphlet do not necessarily represent the total views in respect of the miners' strike of the names of organisations listed below, they consider that the arguments and historical accounts contained within it merit urgent consideration by the British people in general and in particular throughout the membership of the Labour and Trades Union Movement.

The Campaign Group of Labour MPs

National Justice for Mineworkers Campaign

Campaign for Labour Party Democracy

Labour Left Coordinating Committee

Women Against Pit Closures

National Miners' Support Group Committee

Miners' Support Groups (see list on page 61)

First published 1986
Verso 15 Greek Street London W1
© National Justice for Mineworkers Campaign 1986

Designed by Sandra Buchanan
ISBN 0 86091 999 4

Printed and bound by CPI Group (UK) Ltd, Croydon, CR0 4YY

Contents

Preface

THE MINERS' STRIKE 1984-85 was the most honourable strike this century. It was not about money but about people fighting for their jobs, communities and the future of their children. Although the establishment used every weapon at its disposal to crush them, the men, women and children of the mining communities, carried on the struggle for a full year. The Labour Movement must never forget or diminish the historic battle waged by the miners. All of the in-depth academic analysis that has proliferated since the end of the strike has obscured one vital fact – that the leadership of the Labour Movement and the TUC did not deliver the necessary industrial support needed to defeat the Tory Government and the National Coal Board.

There can be no doubt that one of Mrs. Thatcher's major aims from the moment she assumed office was to destroy the Trade Union Movement and above all one of the most powerful trade unions in Britain, the National Union of Mineworkers. She wanted revenge for the magnificent victories of 1972 and 1974 and was prepared to go to any lengths to provoke and break the 1984 strike. In addition to using the police as her private army, she used the courts as an arm of her political policy to sequestrate the NUM's funds and bankrupt the Union at a stroke. The mobilisation of financial support for the NUM from all sectors of the Labour movement enabled the miners to conduct their strike and to feed themselves and their families but the union has still not been able to pay its bills, affiliation fees or staff for over a year because of the sequestration. Socialists should learn the lesson of the sequestration to turn the tables on the establishment in the future. The next labour government should have an official sequestrator to bring back all the tax-avoiding investment which has gone abroad since the Tories took office. All this money should be taxed properly in order to pay for the National Health Service and pensions. If the political will is there this idea can be implemented and a Labour sequestrator can be used to benefit the working class. Perhaps the Tories will then have second thoughts about using this weapon against trade unions again.

The Tories continue to talk about the violence on the picket lines believing that with the acquiescence of their lap-dogs in the media, the public will continue to swallow the propaganda churned out against the NUM leadership and its members. What about the violence of this Tory government? The real violence in this society should be exposed. It is not being perpetrated by people on picket lines fighting to save their jobs but by a heartless Tory government which allows thousands of people to die every year of kidney failure because of the lack of NHS funds. Despite the fiddling of figures and the blatant lies of a Secretary of State for Social Services who does the bidding of a Prime Minister who receives private medical treatment, patients on waiting lists are dying of heart disease, babies are dying of bone marrow disease, women are dying of cervical cancer and research is being criminally curtailed because no money is made available.

Margaret Thatcher's appointment of Ian MacGregor signalled that she was determined to decimate the mining industry. The closure of pits predicted prior to and during the course of the strike is now a reality and the term 'uneconomic' is one that has been used to shut down still viable collieries throughout the British coalfields. Nowhere is the government's stinking hypocracy more obvious than in its use of this bogus term especially when they have bailed out their friends in the city at Johnson Matthey Bankers with over £100m of taxpayers' money and no receivers have been sent in! The Export Credit Guarantee Department, the government's insurance company which insures British exporters against non-payment by foreign buyers, was bankrupt at the end of the last financial year and again Mrs. Thatcher dipped into the taxpayers' pockets to the tune of £350m to save this uneconomic unit of production. The most 'uneconomic' pit of all is the common market, a bottomless pit of bureaucracy, waste and high-living which has just been given £252m worth of British taxpayers' money to balance its books. Whilst Thatcher and her ministers whined on during the strike about the necessity of competing in the marketplace of the 'real world', they provided the farmers with a £2,000m subsidy in 1984 – each farmer averaged a £40,000 payment – all courtesy of the British taxpayer. The double standards of this Tory mob know no bounds when they are defending their own.

The Justice for Mineworkers Campaign has been organised to ensure that *our* own will not be forgotten. There is a great necessity to keep the resolutions adopted by the TUC and Labour Party Conferences in the forefront of the Labour and Trade Union Movement whilst even one worker remains sacked or imprisoned as a result of victimisation for participating in the strike. We ask for the dedicated support of all socialists to make certain that the sacrifices made by working people and in particular the miners and their families are repaid in full.

Dennis Skinner MP

Introduction

THE ADOPTION of the resolutions moved by the National Union of Mineworkers at the 1985 TUC Congress and Labour Party Conference, depite opposition from unsympathetic forces within both of these organisations, has been a massive boost in the campaign to bring to the attention of the public the gross injustice suffered by members of the NUM and their union throughout the fifty-one weeks of the dispute which ended in March 1985.

Such were the feelings within the mining communities against police oppression and the diabolical unfairness of treatment by the courts, that a campaign, consisting of Labour MP's and Labour Party and trade union activists was set up to bring to the attention of the public, instances of illegal police practice, injustices in the courts, infringements of civil liberties, together with the intimidatory attitude of the National Coal Board towards miners who they sacked for either trivial, alleged and in some cases non-existent offences. This book is, therefore, an attempt to pursue a campaign to press for the alleviation of all victimised miners.

The need for such a campaign is clear, especially in respect of reinstatement, for it can be seen that despite the fact that the Parliamentary Select Committee on Employment endorsed the case of the NUM against the Coal Board and proved beyond any shadow of a doubt that various areas were acting differently and where it was obvious from statistical information and reports from the various areas that Scotland, Kent and the North East were facing the most difficulty in getting the NCB to even review cases. Further the need for a campaign is conclusively expressed by the fact that the Coal Board have moved only marginally following the report's publication, have made it obvious that they are only paying lip service to the so-called reviews they promised to carry out in all areas, into all cases.

The publication of this document and the mounting of a national campaign therefore is helping to fulfil the promise to miners made by the National Union of Mineworkers and others in the Trade Union and Labour movement during the course of the dispute, that if they fell foul of either the law or their employer, the NCB, then everything would be done to try and ensure that they did not suffer any hardship.

To this end the Miners Solidarity Fund has been a tremendous assistance to those worst affected, insomuch as it has helped the sacked men and indeed the families of those incarcerated in jail to live at a reasonable standard. However, in view of the fact that the Government and the NCB have made little effort to reinstate miners and continues to victimise them this makes the continuing provision of finance of paramount importance, together with other activities which will highlight their plight and the injustices to them and their families.

There may be those in the movement who see the continued provision of finance as perhaps being a panacea aimed at sweeping the problem to one side, but of course it is nothing of the sort. It is and has been a genuine attempt by responsible people to try and ease hardship and this coupled with the fact that despite the strenuous efforts of the NUM many striking miners remain victimised, the movement must accept an obligation to look after the welfare of victimised miners and their families.

It is therefore commonly accepted that NUM members were deliberately victimised in order to try and weaken the union during and since the strike. The collapse of the riot trials at Orgreave and Mansfield, make it increasingly obvious that many decisions to prosecute and indeed decisions to jail men were based more on politics than on any search for justice.

The Justice for Mineworkers Campaign is thus an attempt to ensure that these and other related matters are constantly brought before the public eye, in an attempt to try and obtain further assistance politically from those within the Trade Union and Labour movement who are sympathetic to the NUM and its members, to try and transform the TUC and Labour Party decisions into positive plans of action leading up to a demand for a full amnesty for all those involved.

It is therefore essential that the information contained within this pamphlet is circulated within the Trade Union and Labour movement and to the general public at large, pointing out the disparities of treatment to sacked miners in different areas of the National Coal Board; pointing out the unjust ways the courts interpreted the law when dealing with strikers, and seeking at all times to ensure that enough money can be collected to prevent these victimised miners from becoming destitute as well as being martyrs.

The Justice for Mineworkers Campaign can only succeed with a broad range of support, it therefore intends to try and seek the assistance of more Labour MP's, more people within the Trade Union movement, the various Womens Support Groups who have continued to do such a splendid job since the end of the dispute in campaigning against pit closures, and campaigning for the reinstatement of sacked miners. It is also intended to try and organise meetings where victimised miners can explain their personal circumstances to the public in some detail to engender further support. This publication is therefore designed to aid their actions.

Only by continuing to highlight the injustices which took place during and since the strike, can the arguments be put for the men, women and families affected to be treated fairly as their only crime, if indeed it was such, was to fight for their jobs, industry and communities.

Bill Etherington

1 History of the strike

WHEN does the history of the miners' strike really start? There are many factors which contributed to the complex situation preceding the strike.

Does it start with the Ridley Plan in 1977 – the plan in which Nicholas Ridley set out the guidelines for a future conservative government to take on the trade unions, the weakest first, the strongest last? Much of the detail of the strategy we saw in the miners' strike – the use of the police, the use of lorries to transport coal – was pre-figured in the Ridley Plan.

Or does the history of the strike really start with the election of the Tories in 1979? Or with the infamous cabinet minute shortly afterwards, which spoke of the ability to massively increase reliance on nuclear power in order to minimise the industrial and political strength of the National Union of Mineworkers? Was the strike the inevitable Tory revenge for their defeats at the hands of the miners in 1972 and 1974?

Could the strike really be traced back to the election of Arthur Scargill as President of the NUM – an almost unique trade union leader whose commitment to fight for the policies of the NUM Conference was utterly unswerving?

Many people would say that the setbacks suffered by other major trade unions – the steel workers, ASLEF over flexible rostering, the Health Service workers, and the NGA in the Warrington Messenger dispute – gave the clear indication that neither the TUC leadership nor the Parliamentary Opposition had recognised the outright confrontation being provoked by the government nor had the guts to stand up to it. Moreover, the experience of the trial runs in those disputes showed that the use of the police and the courts against working people would be grudgingly tolerated by some of the Labour movement's leadership. It could be argued that it was then inevitable that Mrs Thatcher would see the NUM as a prize to be coveted and the stronghold of the miners as a bastion to be stormed.

Or could one identify the appointment of Ian MacGregor as the moment at which the strike became inevitable? Given his record at British Leyland (appointed by a Labour government) and later at the British Steel Corporation, it was quite clear that he was appointed by the Prime Minister as Chairman of the National Coal Board with a mandate to butcher the mining industry.

In an immediate sense, the strike was provoked with MacGregor's announcement that another 4 million tonnes of capacity – leading to a loss of 20,000 jobs – was to be taken out of the industry, and then announcements of the closure of Cortonwood Colliery and the four other pits under immediate threat at that time, without reference to established procedure for closures.

No-one should have been surprised at this development. Arthur Scargill had repeatedly warned of the government's intentions and of the NCB hit lists, and he was right.

Indeed, it is instructive to note how many times what appeared to be key Government and NCB arguments against the NUM subsequently turned out to be issues on which the NUM was proved correct. One only has to trace the propaganda offensive that accompanied the NACODS 'agreement', with Mrs Thatcher and Peter Walker continually urging the NUM to settle on a similar basis. But the NACODS leadership rapidly recognized that their agreement was worthless. And in the spate of pit closures which followed the end of the strike, none was subjected to the new independent review procedure which had been hailed as a great breakthrough by the Government in the NACODS agreement.

Or as another example of the way in which propaganda was used in a blatant attempt to shape the popular view of the dispute, one can trace the television and newspaper hysteria surrounding the long struggle to successfully picket Orgreave. There was daily coverage of hysterical statements from Thatcher, Walker and any number of Tory backbench MPs castigating the pickets, as the organised police thuggery, based on their new Manual of Procedures, went on day after day – unmentioned by the media. But we now know a later chapter in that history has been the acquittal of almost every miner arrested, with many not even facing trial because the police were forced to withdrew charges. We now know that the television news bulletins were blatantly doctored to give the opposite impression to what in fact took place.

An even longer historical memory will find it staggering that the Tory inspired issue of a ballot could be turned into such a serious matter by the NCB and the government – and unfortunately by some leading members of the Labour Party¯ and that it could be used by Mrs Thatcher's friendly Tory judges as a basis for Common Law decisions against the NUM at National and Area levels. All this despite the fact that under Joe Gormley's leadership, the National Executive of the union defied a National Conference decision and a national ballot that went overwhelmingly against productivity deals, and allowed the Nottinghamshire Area to negotiate such a deal with the NCB. And all this despite the fact that a High Court judge had responded to the South Wales and Kent Areas of the union by ruling that ballots and conference decisions in no way bound the union's executive.

Any serious study of the strike will have to conclude that the strike was not about ballots, not about violence, not about trade unions and the law, but about jobs and communities. In a sense, it was remarkable that so many could struggle for so long and for no gain to themselves. It was not a selfish strike, but one based on the finest principles of the stong defending the weak. And as time passes, it becomes increasingly more obvious that the miners were right to make their stand; week by week, it becomes increasingly more apparent that it is the clear intention of the NCB and the government to achieve the destruction of the mining industry, the miners' union and in turn to deal a mortal blow to organised resistance by working people to their policies of the New Right.

And no historical view could fail to observe the unique situation of a major national trade union being put into Receivership, deprived of all its funds, and operating for over a year on the basis of goodwill and donations from sympathisers and supporters in the Labour Movement. The ability of a Conservative government to get away with such a threatened elimination of its opponents will be something which for many years to come will lead people to ask why the wider trade union and Labour movement could have allowed such things to happen without retaliation.

Before the miners' strike, there was a view that was becoming increasingly fashionable, particularly among those who talk of a re-alignment of the Left, that class struggle was a thing of the past.

Scargill and lobby after the NUM executive meeting in Sheffield, 8 March 1984.
John Sturrock/Network

We even heard it said that the present generation of industrial workers, including miners, many with mortgages, hire purchase commitments, foreign holidays and cars, would never again endure a strike of such length and proportions. The miners' strike showed that such a view was nonsense. Not only did the miners themselves, particularly the younger miners, show an almost historically unparalleled determination to win, but another remarkable phenomenon of the strike was the equal determination of the women of the mining communities to participate shoulder to shoulder with their men-folk. If the Labour Party and the TUC were to learn that lesson and to understand that the best hope for the return of a Labour government and the transformation of Britain into a

Socialist society is still the commitment to those in active struggle, then future historians will record that the 1984-85 miners' strike was the beginning of the end of the Thatcher government and all that it stood for. The miners showed that resistance is possible and the determined manner in which resistance would be crushed by a Tory Party intent on maintaining the last vestiges of a capitalist society. Other working people must now join that resistance and ensure the irreversible transformation of society to one based on the commonwealth of working people and their families.

2 Chronology of the strike

THE EVENTS leading to the overtime ban in November 1983 and the subsequent miners' strike for jobs in 1984-85.

27 SEPTEMBER 1983 NUM submits annual pay claim.

29 SEPTEMBER 1983 NCB gives written negative reply to the Union's claim, adding that before their offer of a 5.2% could be accepted: *"first over-production of high cost capacity must be eliminated"*.

21 OCTOBER 1983 NUM Special Delegate Conference unanimously agreed:
1) to reject the Board's wage proposals as totally unsatisfactory;
2) to reaffirm the Union's opposition to pit closures other than on grounds of exhaustion and to fight any further reduction in manpower levels and to resist NCB/Government plans to close 70 pits over the coming five year period;
3) to impose a full overtime ban from 31st October.

27 OCTOBER 1983 NCB reaffirms their demands.

31 OCTOBER 1983 Overtime ban started.

1 MARCH 1984 NCB announces the closure of Cortonwood Colliery in Yorkshire and announce a cut back of 4 million tonnes of coal in the forthcoming year with a loss of 20,000 jobs.

5 MARCH 1984   Strike starts in Yorkshire in protest, following an overwhelming mandate for a ballot vote to take industrial action to protect jobs and mining communities.

6 MARCH 1984   Scottish and Yorkshire Areas of the NUM call strike action. By 12th March half of the miners on strike nationally.

14 MARCH 1984   The National Reporting Centre, at the request of the Nottingham Police drafts 8,000 police officers into the county from half of the 43 forces in Britain. Court rules that Yorkshire NUM must withdraw flying pickets.

15 MARCH 1984   David Jones, miner aged 23, killed whilst picketing in Ollerton, Notts.

18 MARCH 1984   Kent miners stopped by police and turned back at the Dartford Tunnel. Police occupy army camps in Nottinghamshire.

19 MARCH 1984   Yorkshire NUM arising from litigation under Tory anti-trade union legislation found to be in contempt of court (postponed indefinitely). NUM members picket 27 Notts pits and peacefully persuade their colleagues to join the strike action. Police decide to blockade the county of Nottinghamshire.

26 MARCH 1984   Lancashire NUM joins strike. A. Scargill appears in High Court fighting to ensure investment of NUM pension funds in Britain.

28 MARCH 1984   Yorkshire miners block a section of the M1 motorway.

29 MARCH 1984   Transport unions impose ban on the movement of coal, partially successfully. Nurses join the picket lines in South Wales.

3-9 APRIL 1984   Food kitchens open in every coalfield.

10 APRIL 1984   Emergency debate in the House of Commons on the role of the police in the strike.

11 APRIL 1984   Pit Deputies vote to join strike.

19 APRIL 1984   NUM Special Conference ratifies strike action in the Areas and calls on all miners to rally to the defence of their industry.

20 APRIL 1984   Notts and Midlands NUM decide to join strike.

26 APRIL 1984   High Court says No to NUM policy on investment of pension funds in Britain.

2 MAY 1984   CEGB figures show more oil being used to counterbalance coal shortage.

4 MAY 1984   Didcot and Aberthaw power stations shut down.

17 MAY 1984   Leon Brittan admits in Parliament plain clothes police operating in Notts coalfield.

23 MAY 1984   NCB walks out of talks with NUM and demand pledge of union co-operation in the closing of 'uneconomic pits'.

25 MAY 1984   Full-scale picketing at the Orgreave coke works. Nottinghamshire scab miners obtain a court order which allows them to continue working, but which declares that those on strike were striking officially.

29 MAY 1984   Approximately 2,000 police use riot gear, horses and baton charges to take coke lorries through picket lines into Orgreave, even though coke workers join picket line.

30 MAY 1984   Major confrontations at the Orgreave picket. 82 arrests including A. Scargill, 62 injured.

31 MAY 1984   Approximately 3,200 police in riot gear at Orgreave from 13 area police forces force major confrontation with unarmed strikers.

31 MAY 1984   Further conflict at Orgreave. 19 arrests, 20 people injured including 5 police officers.

7 JUNE 1984   Commons debate on the miners strike. Thousands march to lobby Parliament. 100 arrests.

8-13 JUNE 1984   Talks with NCB, which again result in demands on NUM to agree to management strategy.

15 JUNE 1984   Joe Green, miner, crushed to death on picket duty at Ferry Bridge.

18 JUNE 1984   The battle of Orgreave, where police run amok. 93 arrests, many miners injured including A. Scargill.

27 JUNE 1984   Over 50,000 people march in support of the NUM. NCB announces switch of movement of coal from rail to road.

1 JULY 1984   Leon Brittan endorses use of Criminal Law rather than Civil Law against the miners.

5 JULY 1984   NCB/NUM talks, agreed to talk again.

6 JULY 1984   NCB management visits NUM members at home encouraging them back to work.

8 JULY 1984   High Court declares NUM Annual Conference unlawful. National dock strike called against the movement of coal.

13 JULY 1984   Government withholds tax refunds to striking miners.

John Sturrock/Network

19 JULY 1984 NUM/NCB talks last 3 days. Despite NUM willingness to negotiate, the NCB are ordered to stand firm.

31 JULY 1984 South Wales NUM fined £50,000 under Tory anti-trade union legislation on picketing.

8 AUGUST 1984 Trades Unions press for a 50p a week levy in support of NUM. MacGregor writes to all striking miners urging a return to work.

11 AUGUST 1984 Petition handed to the Queen on the plight of striking miners and their families.

13 AUGUST 1984 Police refuse to co-operate with the National Council for Civil Liberties re. policing of the strike.

16 AUGUST 1984 South Wales NUM found in contempt of court for refusing to pay fine in line with TUC Wembley Conference policy. £770,000 of their funds seized. NCB warns of large job losses in mining due to pits deteriorating.

23 AUGUST 1984 MacGregor offers working miners 5.2% increase if they agree to work overtime.

24 AUGUST 1984 Second dock strike called following the unloading of coal at Hunterstone.

3 SEPTEMBER 1984 TUC pledges support for the NUM.

12 SEPTEMBER 1984 TUC attempts to organise talks between the NUM and the NCB. NACODS ballot to strike over instructions to cross picket lines.

18 SEPTEMBER 1984 Three-week dock strike called off.

26 SEPTEMBER 1984 NCB offers NACODS compromise package.

28 SEPTEMBER 1984 High Court rules that NUM cannot be forced to hold national ballot. NACODS ballot result announced – 82.5% majority for strike.

29 SEPTEMBER 1984 NCB/NUM agree to hold separate exploratory talks.

1 OCTOBER 1984 Overwhelming support for the NUM at the Labour Party Conference, whilst NUM/NACODS meet NCB. President served with a High Court writ whilst sitting in the NUM delegation. The NEC of the NUM reaffirm that the strike action was official despite court decision.

2 OCTOBER 1984 NUR/ASLEF members sent home for refusing to move coal.

4 OCTOBER 1984 Depite NUM lawyers arguing that the case

should go to a full trial the High Court gives NUM 5 days to obey the interlocutory injunction and to call the strike off.

8 OCTOBER 1984 NUM/NCB agree to meet at ACAS under independent Chair on 11 October.

10 OCTOBER 1984 NUM fined £200,000 and found in contempt of High Court.

11 OCTOBER 1984 ACAS talks begin, although Ian MacGregor declares of ACAS 'This place stinks' and continues to demand NUM concessions.

12 OCTOBER 1984 Restrictive bail conditions on striking members upheld in the Divisional Courts.

15 OCTOBER 1984 Despite NUM willing to accept two formulas put forward by ACAS, the negotiations are terminated when NCB walk out.

17 OCTOBER 1984 NACODS call strike for 25th October.

20 OCTOBER 1984 Michael Eaton replaces MacGregor in NCB public relations role.

25 OCTOBER 1984 ACAS prepare formula which both NACODS and NUM accept, which includes provision for independent review procedure – NCB continue their demands on NUM and despite TUC advice NACODS call off strike. Courts attempt to seize £200,000 NUM funds.

26 OCTOBER 1984 NUM rejects NCB demands. High Court orders total sequestration of NUM funds.

28 OCTOBER 1984 Court moves to makes 24 members of the NUM executive liable for the £200,000 contempt fine.

1 NOVEMBER 1984 MacGregor says: 'There is no basis for further talks with the NUM'.

2 NOVEMBER 1984 NCB offers miners a back to work cash bonus.

4 NOVEMBER 1984 Sequestrator obtains an injunction from Irish Judge on a Sunday afternoon in his home to freeze NUM funds deposited in Eire.

5 NOVEMBER 1984 Legal action sought in the High Court to prevent Yorkshire Area NUM officers from control of their funds.

7 NOVEMBER 1984 NUM resist Sequestrator's application to return union assets to UK and Dublin Court rules £2.75 million NUM funds remain frozen and not given to Sequestrator.

10 NOVEMBER 1984 Transport unions call on international support to mount blockade of coal and oil shipments to the UK.

11 NOVEMBER 1984 NCB offers £650 Christmas bonus to striking miners who return to work by 19th November.

17 NOVEMBER 1984 NCB refuses to negotiate unless NUM gives agreement to close pits.

21 NOVEMBER 1984 Government increases deduction of supplementary benefits to £16 per week for strikers' families.

28 NOVEMBER 1984 TUC General Council seeks talks with government over Miners strike.

30 NOVEMBER 1984 Arising out of failure to seize the Union's overseas assets a Receiver appointed to control NUM assets and funds. Mr. Brewer, a Tory Party official from Derbyshire starts his abortive trek to get NUM money.

5 DECEMBER 1984 MacGregor announces plans to privatise pits.

9 DECEMBER 1984 Receiver and Sequestrator try to seize £4.6 million NUM funds from Luxembourg but again the NUM application successfully freezes the account.

17 DECEMBER 1984 MacGregor dashes TUC peace hopes.

12 JANUARY 1985 Henry Richardson – pro-strike leader Notts NUM – suspended from office.

22 JANUARY 1985 Challenge to the government's right to deduct £16 from supplementary benefits paid to striking miners' families. Failed in the High Court.

23 JANUARY 1985 Peter Walker, Secretary of State for Energy, refuses to hold an independent inquiry into the future of the coal industry. NUM General Secretary, Peter Heathfield, meets with NCB Director for informal discussions but MacGregor intervenes to prevent negotiations.

29 JANUARY 1985 NCB insists upon the precondition that NUM sign agreement not to oppose pit closures.

1 FEBRUARY 1985 Full hearing of case starts in Dublin High Court on possession of £2.7 million of NUM funds frozen by earlier court order.

8 FEBRUARY 1985 Joint appeal by NUM and NACODS to reopen talks.

13 FEBRUARY 1985 High Court order approved banning mass picketing in Yorkshire pits.

22 FEBRUARY 1985 TUC initiative to end strike fails.

24 FEBRUARY 1985 Mass rally in London – many arrests.

28 FEBRUARY 1985 MacGregor pledges that sacked miners will not be re-employed.

3 MARCH 1985 NUM ends strike. A Special Delegate Conference votes by 98-91 to return to work on 5th March 1985 without an agreement.

5 MARCH 1985 Kent miners stay in strike and continue to picket other coalfields to demand amnesty for sacked miners.

8 MARCH 1985 Kent miners return to work.

22 MAY 1985 NUM appears before Select Committee of the House of Commons on Employment. The Committee required the NCB to review all cases of sacked miners.

18 JUNE 1985 Irish High Court dismisses Sequestrator's application to return NUM funds to Britain.

1 SEPTEMBER 1985 TUC Congress adopts resolution calling for a campaign for the re-instatement of victimised miners and repayment of the fine costs of NUM relating to sequestration and receivership.

1 OCTOBER 1985 Labour Party Conference adopts a composite resolution calling for repayment of cost of sequestration and a campaign for victimised miners.

28 OCTOBER 1985 NUM holds Special Delegate Conference in London and agrees to support a campaign for all sacked/victimised miners as a result of the dispute.

3 The financial hijack of the Union

FOLLOWING the 1985 Labour Party Conference decision in October and that of the TUC Congress earlier in the year which adopted resolutions which paid tribute to the heroic struggle of the NUM, it was recognised that they had been attacked by the power of the state via sequestration and the imposition of a receiver.

Conference called on the next Labour government to review all cases of miners jailed as a result of the dispute, reinstate all sacked miners and reimburse the union of all monies confiscated as a result of fines, sequestration and receivership.

Some people may now be wondering why, when one recalls the degree of rank and file unity during the strike, it became necessary to embody such a commitment at all.

The reason is as simple as it was straightforward to the many affiliated trades unions/organisations and CLP delegates who supported the resolution whilst attending the conferences, that the way in which the NUM fought for their jobs and communities against the state apparatus was an example to them all and in the best traditions of trade union history on behalf of their memberships.

The situation now

The Leaders of the National Union of Mineworkers may now face action to establish personal liability for over £1 million charged by sequestrators and the Receiver.

Their alleged crime? Carrying out the decisions of the NUM National Executive Committee, delegate conference and their members.

Not one penny was paid to the NUM from November 1984, when, by the decision of a High Court judge, acting on the complaint of a handful of opponents of the democratic decisions of the union – with the connivance of those concerned in the sequestration – the entire union's assets were placed in the hands of a Receiver.

The union's crime? Carrying out the democratic decisions of the overwhelming majority of its members, in accordance with union rules.

Even though the original case against the union, which had resulted in Sequestration, had been abandoned, and its authors supported the claim for the union to have its funds back, the NUM's assets were still under the control of the state-appointed Receiver. He is Michael Arnold, of the Arthur Young firm of accountants, whose association with the Johnson Matthey Bank have led to other problems.

Arnold filed a writ on 19 September 1985 against the NUM president, Arthur Scargill, NUM general secretary, Peter Heathfield, and NUM vice-president, Michael McGahey. Such are the powers assumed by the Receiver, that the writ was actually filed in the name of the NUM. As far as the courts are concerned, this unelected man *is* the NUM.

A judge had thus removed the trustees of the union's funds, replaced them with a man able first to pay himself and the sequestrators out of those funds, and then accuse the original trustees of being liable for these costs.

Without funds, the union has been unable to pay TUC affiliation fees, Labour Party affiliation fees, and has had no money to campaign for the retention of the political fund. The Receiver paid no wages to NUM head office staff, nor pensions to retired staff, and met no bills. The union itself cannot buy stationery, paper or pay for printing.

The NUM has been unable to adequately finance its normal operations on behalf of its members – even though they are paying their subscriptions every week through deductions which the Coal Board hands directly to the Receiver, with the Receiver claiming he has such draconian powers that the TUC would be subject to a writ if it set up a trust fund to meet liabilities of the NUM. He has tried to deter people who wanted to give assistance by threatening them with contempt of court.

South Africa

Further worrying is the fact that, despite the NUM's well-known policy of non-investment of assets in South African companies, the Receiver has shown complete disregard by depositing £4.7 million of the sequestrated funds in Standard Chartered Bank, whose South African subsidiary, Standard Bank, currently has assets of over 16,100 billion Rand (£7 billion) in South Africa and whose annual accounts reveal that it derived 29% of its group profit from South Africa during 1984.

Trade union law

What also was apparently little known was that until the 1974 Labour Government's Trade Union and Labour Relations Act, such an attack on a union by a receiver would have been impossible. This is because, in scouring the legal texts, lawyers hostile to the NUM had discovered that, when drafting the Bill, the Labour government had as confirmed by the lawyers responsible, inadvertently removed an immunity for trades unions which had previously existed for decades. This allowed for the first time a receiver to be appointed over the funds of a union.

It has, therefore, legitimately been argued by the NUM, that because of this blunder, the Labour Party had a particular responsibility to rectify the effects caused by this omission, especially as what lay behind this legal straitjacket was a Tory conspiracy of international dimensions, the lessons of which are ignored by the labour and trade union movement at its peril.

Background

To understand this, one must recall the events leading up to and since the legal moves on sequestration and receivership.

In the autumn of 1984 the legal attack on the NUM swung into action in earnest. Shortly after the NACODS pit deputies leaders decided against calling their members out on strike, legal moves intitiated in early August were brought rapidly to a head.

Like every court action in which the NUM had been involved since the start of the strike, its outcome was unfavourable to the union. Two miners from Yorkshire sought to have the strike in their area ruled unofficial. The national union became involved since its NEC had sanctioned the area strike under rule.

When the High Court injunction was given against the union, the NEC and subsequently a special delegates' conference decided that to comply with the court was to violate both the spirit and the letter of the union's rules and the principles of the TUC Wembley Conference. They were obliged to reject the injunction. Although representatives of 200,000 miners, acting democratically, rejected the verdict of a single, unelected judge, they were deemed to be outside the law of the land.

On 10 October 1984, Mr. Justice Nicholls ordered the union to pay a fine of £200,000. On 25 October, when the fine had not been paid, the High Court appointed sequestrators to seize *all* union assets.

The sequestrators proved unable to retrieve the money which the union had invested abroad. But soon after the foreign courts told sequestrators they were not recognised to have rights to the funds, a new High Court action suddenly appeared.

A string of plaintiffs named in the writ was headed by Colin Clarke, known for his activities on behalf of the anti-strike National Working Miners' Committee. Clarke's legal representatives demanded something which no English court had ever been asked to consider before – the appointment of a receiver over the union's funds through the removal of its trustees.

The suspicions of the union were aroused by a bizarre intervention in the Clarke case by representatives of the sequestrators. During an out-of-court meeting on 30 November 1984, lawyers for Clarke had agreed with lawyers for the NUM to drop the demand for a receiver. Provided a written undertaking was given by the NUM that the money would not be moved, Clarke's lawyers were satisfied. But as the judge was preparing to hear the terms of the agreement, a barrister spoke out from the back of the court. He told the judge he represented the sequestrators and wished to address the court.

Despite the fact that the sequestrators were not parties to the court case, and had no right of intervention, the judge permitted him to speak. The barrister denounced the out-of-court agreement, encouraging the judge to appoint a receiver.

The judge did just that – despite the fact that the two parties to the dispute had already settled it to their own mutual satisfaction. Justice Mervyn Davies sacked the union's three elected trustees, and appointed a Tory activist from Derbyshire, Herbert Brewer, as receiver.

The union immediately went to the Court of Appeal. They argued that such an appointment had never happened before, and even in cases of receivership over companies, a shareholder must first raise the issue at shareholders' meetings before resorting to legal action. The appeal was thrown out. Although the original plaintiffs had agreed that a receiver was not necessary, the union's funds were now firmly under his control.

Several months later on 17 June, 1985, during a Dublin High Court ruling opposing the claim of the Receiver to NUM funds held in the Republic of Ireland, a certain Justice Barrington commented that: '. . . it would appear that the idea of appointing a receiver came from Continental lawyers engaged in attempting to trace the Union's assets and not because of any difficulties peculiar to the Irish litigation.'

Certainly, Clarke's lawyers were not understood to be trying to 'trace' union assets, so who was the Irish judge referring to? This 'idea' of receivership appears to have been quite remarkably passed to them from the Continent – a case of legal telepathy!

NUM v. State

Thus emerged the gradual acceptance of the sequestrators acting on behalf of the British state, and with it a recognition by politicians and bankers alike of the immediate dangers of handing over a client's cash to a foreign state-appointed receiver acting on what was widely seen on the Continent as a political motive, this undoubtedly being the reason why judges in Ireland and in Luxembourg refused to release accredited funds.

Since the end of the strike the NUM complied with the two original conditions of the British High Court which were to return its funds to Britain and place them in the hands of the receiver/sequestrator and to appoint new trustees. Since then, the original case by the two Yorkshire miners, Robert Taylor and Ken Foulstone, the latter currently serving a jail sentence for burglary, was abandoned. But although the original grounds for sequestration and receivership were removed, the High Court firstly refused to bring forward their hearing set for 3 October and then postponed a hearing on the receivership to a later date after the sequestration order was considered.

What is abundantly clear from this is that the State itself was standing in the way of the return of the union's funds. Further, it is possible that the High Court-appointed officials' action in taking out a personal liability action on 19 September 1985 against the union's three principal leaders will tie up union's funds for months. Once again, it is important to consider the timing of their actions. It followed the withdrawal of the original case which had given rise to the sequestration order and it came in the midst of the NUM struggle to defend itself against a breakaway organisation.

Yet, despite the exhausting work of locating union funds and paying over £1 million of it to virtually no-one but themselves, the receiver and the sequestrators had been very responsive to demands from the Nottinghamshire NUM.

While the national union had been deprived of funds to put its case to miners in the area, Notts NUM received full payment of staff wages, general upkeep, and even money for the publication of area propaganda material – though areas, in accordance with union rule, had to finance that type of publicity work themselves.

End of sequestration

The two original plaintiffs in the case which had led to the sequestration of the NUM's assets, Taylor and Foulstone, withdrew proceedings and abandoned their case with an undertaking to support an application for the removal of the Order of Sequestration. The strike having been over for some six months and therefore any question of whether it was called official or not being purely academic, the National Executive Committee of the union instructed that the union's alleged Contempt of Court be purged and that the Sequestration Order be lifted. This was heard before Justice Nicholls on 14 November 1985, and despite his criticism of the 'perfunctory' apology made on behalf of the union the judge discharged the sequestrator and ordered that their not inconsiderable costs be met out of the NUM funds.

The whole NUM National Executive Committee attended the Court and thereby indicated their solidarity both with all the actions which had been undertaken on behalf of the union and in their wish to restore financial control of the union back to its members. Just as the strike had ended in March in a dignified manner and with heads held high so the NEC went to the court not with remorse for the decisions that they had taken and not accepting defeat but intent on regaining control of their union in the best interests of the industry and the membership.

The Order of Receivership however continued to remain in force although the orginal requirement of the court had long been met. Three new trustees had been appointed who appeared to satisfy the court as to their credentials, the union's funds had been returned to the UK and all the assurances required to end the receivership had been given.

There is no doubt that it was the Receivership Order which had been both the most pernicious and problematic for the NUM, made more bitter by the fact that it was as a result of the 1974 Labour government's legislation that had in the first place given an opportunity for a receiver to be appointed to any union. Whilst we must continue to oppose Tory laws which are clearly intended to cripple the Trade Union movement, as Socialists we must also ensure as far as possible that any new legislation introduced by the next Labour government cannot be abused by our opponents, or otherwise be prepared, should that be the case, to grant immunity and if necessary retrospective compensation as a matter of principle.

There may be some who would say that the elaborate steps taken by the NUM to safe-guard their funds achieved little. But just as the greatest significant of the twelve month strike was the very fact that it took place at all and in the process created an awareness amongst countless working people that resistance is still possible, so it cannot be forgotten that the whole power of the State never succeeded in its intention to smash the NUM and never stopped the union from functioning for even one day. The power of the State, combined with both overt and covert co-operation from the capitalist system, cannot defeat the strength of combined determination by working people and their leadership to stand up against them. Trade Unions must consider the lessons for the future both in their own investment policy but also by realising that simply to be good managers within the capitalist system is not sufficient. Until Labour has control not only of the means of production but also of the financial institutions we shall be fighting with both arms tied behind our back against the combined strength of capitalism.

These, then, are just some of the details of the state attack on the NUM which was a legalised anti-working class attack of enormous gravity.

4 The attack on civil liberties

IN THEIR frenzy to smash the miners' strike the government judiciary and the police took gigantic steps to reduce the civil liberties of the striking miners and their supporters.

Perhaps the first outrage was the public declaration of the Attorney General Sir Michael Havers on a radio programme that the police had sufficient power to stop pickets travelling to pits if they took the view that a breach of the peace might take place. Within hours of this declaration the Kent police put a road block across the Dartford Tunnel some one-hundred miles away from the closest Midlands pits and stopped any car that looked as if it might be carrying Kent miners, and threatening the men with arrest if they went through the tunnel. After injuction proceedings brought by the Kent NUM, and a considerable protest by the public, the Attorney General remained silent, but the pattern had been set.

From then on massive forces of police blocked various routes from the M1 leading to the Midlands pits and prevented the miners and their supporters from getting anywhere near the pits they wished to picket peacefully. Any foreign visitor driving along the M1 could

John Sturrock/Network

have been forgiven for thinking that they were entering a high security war zone judging by the enormous numbers of police and police vehicles which either blocked the roads, stood parked along the verges or travelled systematically in long convoys from one area to another.

No longer could a miner exercise his lawful right to travel peacefully to any other part of the country without being stopped. No longer could any other man or group of men who looked like miners travel peacefully through the Midlands without being stopped by the police.

The government openly exorted the police to take whatever steps the police thought necessary to stop picketing and enable the few

pits that were still producing coal to continue working. They lavished money on the police despite generally denying there was no money for public expenditure in even the most needy areas of the deprived inner cities. Was there an outcry from the government when one southern constabulary chartered a jet to carry the police from the southern counties to the Midlands for picket duties?

The government carried out an active campaign throughout the media wholly blaming the striking miners for violence on the picket line, as well as totally ignoring the escalating violence in the police and the continuing erosion of the public's rights. Police were encouraged and allowed to use pre-emptive charges by batten swinging police horsemen. They were allowed and encouraged to use snatch squads often of heavily armoured policemen who would force their way into a line of pickets to break up the line and give other constables opportunities to arrest pickets withou reason. Evidence at the Orgreave trial revealed internal police directions which actively encouraged the police officers to use violence when dealing with picketing.

The government assisted in the organisation and paid for the National Reporting Centre, the first attempt in Britain to organise policing on a national strategic level without taking into account any of the needs or views of local inhabitants.

The police for their part generally pursued a vigorous aggressive campaign against striking miners. The policemen on picket duties in many areas were encouraged to view striking miners as the enemy. The frequently used excessive violence on even elderly miners who were arrested for trivial offences and despite the fact that no resistance was offered by the men. The miners were abusedand openly insulted by the police who faced them on the picket lines. these was on prosecution of police officers who were seen to assault pickets, even when clear evidence of the attacks were shown on the television.

The police openly refused to allow pickets to speak peacefully to miners who were going to work. The pickets who managed to get through the road blocks were kept even a half a mile or more away from the pit gate. Gone completely are the days when it was accepted law that a number of pickets could stand across the workplace gate and speak to their fellow workers going into work so as to try to put the striker's point of view. The police developed the tactic of making mass arrests in order to completely remove pickets from the picket line, knowing that the magistrates would impose bail conditions that were so oppressive that the result would be that the men could no longer take part in the strike.

In Colchester the police went even further and arrested pickets who were behaving quite peacefully so as to reduce the number of potential pickets in one area to prevent the possibility of a breach of the peace. The Colchester police had no intention of charging any of these men, and indeed there was no suggestion that any crime had been committed. Nevertheless, the dozen pickets found they were unlawfully imprisoned in a Colchester police garage for a day.

Not satisfied with the Public Order Act offences the police resorted to the ancient crime of watching and besetting under the Conspiracy and Protection of Property Act 1875. Several men, including a passing farmer, were arrested in their pit village in Kent for standing on a street corner talking. All the men were found not guilty by the magistrates, there being no evidence against the defendants. The police rapidly dropped the case against the farmer when they realised their blunder.

The Act was also used against 21 kent miners who were following in their motor cars behind a convoy of four police cars, and an NCB bus. The police alleged that the occupants of the bus were intimidated by the men in the vehicles up to half a mile behind, and out of vision. A novel if not vicious approach by the police. All the men were acquitted.

Perhaps the most serious prosecutions, however, were those in the Midlands and Yorkshire where dozens of miners are accused of unlawful assembly and riot. The evidence when presented by the prosecution was non-existent and exposed an overwhelming prejudice of senior policemen towards the miners on strike. The country now knows from the details of the remaining cases which were dropped by the prosecution that there was no substance in the charges brought against the men who were doing no more than standing up for the jobs of themselves, their workmates and their children.

It has always been a working rule that prosecutions should not be brought unless there is a reasonable prospect of the offence being proved. Indeed the DPP will not prosecute a policeman accused of a crime unless there is more than a 51% chance of the prosecution succeeding. The police during the strike, particularly in relation to the most serious charges, worked on the basis that they should charge the miners on the basis of prejudice, assertions made by Minsters of the government, and senior employees of the NCB and allegations carried by the media.

Pickets have been brought before the magistrates on and off over the years, but the dispute soon saw magistrates setting bail conditions in respect of largely trivial crimes which were so oppressive that even the most conservative of lawyers found them unjustifiable. Indeed, in the early days of the strike the Essex magistates ordered bail restrictions that prevented Kent miners from picketing at any of the three ports in Essex where coal was being imported, even though the alleged offence occurred at only one of the ports. This was despite the fact that some of the alleged offences were no more than sitting down in the road. The magistrates' aim was clearly to drive the miners out of Essex.

The magistrates in Ramsgate who first of all restricted Kent miners from picketing anywhere in Kent, including their own pits went even further in other cases by restricting the men from picketing anywhere at all. These magistrates took it upon themselves to prevent the men from fighting for their jobs. The conditions were so hastily imposed that men found that they were in breach of the conditions by going to the local Tesco's to shop, to their doctors or the hospital and in some instances even to their own homes. One London magistate upon hearing that the accused miner was not a resident in London imposed a condition of bail that he should not come to London for any reason whatsoever.

No matter what arguments were put up by lawyers representing the miners they were not listened to because the magistrates were showing their class colours. In Mansfield the magistrates even had bail notices with bail restrictions pre-printed ready to hand out to the accused miners even before their names were read out in court.

What did the High Court Judges do to prevent this appalling erosion of civil liberties? They stood by and either condoned the erosion without any care whatsoever or formally supported the erosion of liberities in order to supress the miners' strike.

An application for an injunction against the Kent police for blocking the Dartford Tunnel failed. The judge was not sufficiently interested to safeguard the individual's rights to travel peacefully across the country. The applications to the Divisional Court for an order preventing the police road blocks in the Midlands failed, the court endorsing the police action.

The application to the High Court to quash Mansfield's pre-printed bail notices was lost, the judges endorsing the magistrates' actions.

Already the general erosion of civil liberties which occurred during the miners' strike is being felt by the public. There are calls for longer prison sentences by those in power. Magistrates now feel much more ready to impose stringent bail conditions. The police have developed an aggressive mode of dealing with other strikers and dissenters. The Police and Criminal Evidence Act has been passed by Parliament giving the police much wider powers to deal with the public. Plastic bullets and tear gas will be used in inner city disturbances and it will not be long befoe a coach load of CND supporters are prevented from travelling to a demonstation. Those who have fought for civil liberties over the past fifty years are aware of the addage 'give the police an inch and they will take a mile'.

Statistics on arrests

THE total number of arrests up to 5th March 1985 (excluding supporters on street collections) was 11,312.

England and Wales	
Arrests to 5th March 1985	9,808
Cases heard in court to 5th March 1985	5,653
Number of charges	10,372
Persons released without charges	1,891
Acquittals	1,335
Persons charged with an offence	7,917
Cases awaiting court hearing to 5th March 1985	819

Scotland	
Persons charged with an offence	1,483
Acquittals	140
Convicted	603

Complaints against police	
Total up to 26th February 1985	549
Withdrawn	111
Involving assault by police	256

Complaints break-down by police force	
South Yorkshire	231
Derbyshire	67
Nottinghamshire	62
Metropolitan	12

Number of persons who served time in prison or custody — 200 (approx)

Number of persons still in prison at the end of November 1985 — 17

John Sturrock/Network

The role of the judiciary

There is no doubt that arrest and criminal charges where used as a weapon to contain or weaken the strike action. The total number of persons arrested was at least 11,312, of whom some 1,504 were released without any charge whatsoever.

Some other facts:

1) Of those charged less than 9% related to offences against the person and 11% for criminal damage. The vast majority, nearly 70%, had charges brought for obstruction or breach of the peace.

2) Of those sentenced 4.2% received a custodial sentence and the vast majority were fined: 53.6%: or bound over: 30%.

3) Of those charged and who appeared before the Courts, over half were either acquitted or bound over.

4) The use of bail conditions shows that two-thirds had imposed conditional bail upon them and clearly the intention was to restrict their ability to picket or otherwise participate in strike action.

5) Acquittal rates varied area by area and nearly 40% of cases in Nottinghamshire received acquittals, whilst only 20% in South Wales. The decision to make use of stipendiary magistrates was to reduce the acquittal rate to under 30% whereas those acquitted who appeared before lay magistrates was some 36%.

6 Statistics on victimisation

THIS table shows the number of miners remaining sacked out of the total number dismissed in each area as of Nov. 1985.

Area	Total no dismissed for activities in the dispute	No still in prison 30.11.85	No Remaining Dismissed 30.11.85
Cokemen	11	0	10
COSA	0	0	0
Durham	150	3	86
Durham Mechanics	9	0	5
Kent	48	3	48
Leicestershire	0	0	0
Midlands	22	0	21

North Derbyshire	76	3	26
Northumberland	29	1	16
North Wales	0	0	0
North Western	2	0	2
Nottingham	31	0	27
Power Group	2	0	2
Scotland	206	0	153
South Derbyshire	0	0	0
South Wales	74	2	8
Yorkshire	306	5	146
TOTAL	966	17	550

Select Committee on Employment

The National Coal Board in evidence to the House of Commons Select Committee on Employment appearing before them on 22nd May 1985, confirmed that a total number of 995 men were sacked for activities arising out of the strike. That figure is substantially greater than that recorded by the NUM, and the NUM records reflect those sacked from private mines who are not employed by the NCB.

The report of the Select Committee indicated that the NCB had not followed the ACAS Code of Conduct in relation to those dismissals and had agreed that their procedures amounted to 'summary treatment'. It was recommended that the NCB institute a review of all cases at individual level consistent with the spirit and guidelines of the ACAS code.

Strike Related Offences

Only a small number of miners had been dismissed for offences against the person or damage to property. If the NCB criterion for re-employment as laid before the select committee had indeed been followed, it is contended that 90% would have been reinstated. Indeed, some 21 miners cleared by the courts are still not reinstated.

Reinstatement

The vast majority of miners taken back onto colliery books have been re-engaged and only a few reinstated. The NCB have maintained that these matters rest with their area directors. However, the preceding table quite clearly shows the inconsistency of approach. Discussions have finally commenced in Scotland in late October 1985 with 53 miners being either re-engaged or reinstated.

Victimisation for Trade Union Activities

Many of those sacked and not re-employed had been active branch officials and, it is contended, are clear victims of NCB attempts to stifle them, to remove them from the industry and thereby to reduce the effectiveness of the NUM as a trade union.

7 Women's support groups

THE WOMEN of the coalfields have been described as a sleeping giant, roused to action by the threat to their communities and their children's future. Singing, shouting, rattling tins and waving banners, they threw their weight behind the strike.

Their role was crucial in sustaining the strike, in feeding and clothing their people, in keeping up morale and building a sense of community. At the same time, almost without realising it, they found themselves writing a new chapter in the history of women's struggle.

From about three or four weeks into the strike, people started to realise that it was going to be a long one. Women in the villages – relatives, neighbours and friends – started talking among themselves. In some areas, women had already come together over local issues – in Derbyshire women had campaigned for Tony Benn's election, while in Durham women were already involved in the SEAM campaign – so the basis of support groups was already there. Soon miners' wives' support groups were starting up throughout the length and breadth of Britain. There was no centralized directive or overall plan – just groups of women meeting in each others' front rooms with a common purpose: 'We must *do* something to help our community survive.'

Often it was the plight of the single miners which first prompted the women into action. After just two or three weeks with no income whatsoever, many of them were in a sorry state. There were tales of lads surviving on a diet of bar snacks and fainting on picket lines. Families were little better off; a married couple with two children were entitled to just £11.74 a week benefit to live on (a similar couple not on strike would be getting £48.25 a week – the official government 'poverty line').

The government having prepared its ground by passing a law whereby £15 was deducted from any benefit paid to a striker's family – the amoung of pay he was 'deemed' to be getting, even though everyone knew full well that the miners got nothing, and indeed the union's funds were soon to be sequestrated anyway. The saddest cases were the families where both husband and wife worked for the NCB. The hard-heartedness of a government that would see children starve in pursuit of its policies only made the women all the more determined.

There is no doubt that without their magnificent effort, and the generosity and hard work of miners' support groups throughout Britain and overseas, the miners would have been starved back within a few weeks. Trades unions both at home and abroad, the Labour Party and other socialist organisations, community and ethnic groups, lesbian and gay groups, and millions of individuals rallied to the miners' cause. Little groups of people plastered with bright yellow stickers rattling collecting tins became a regular feature in almost every town, (as were the men in blue moving them on or arresting them, with an astonishing grasp of legal complexity – *'you can hold that tin, but not shake it', 'you must seal it with sellotape, not a rubber band', 'you can't put your toes over that line'*

Street collections were never a popular activity. There was always someone who would give you an earful of abuse – but they were the essential life-line of the support groups. And people's generosity often brought tears to the eyes – from the old age pensioner who pulled out a crumpled pound from her purse, and everyone could see it was all she had, to the one of the young woman who wrote a cheque for £100. As well as street collections, the support groups organised a constant programme of fund-raising activities, from concerts and socials to jumble sales and coffee mornings. Everything that could be was auctioned, sold or raffled, everything that moved was sponsored – walks, bed-pushes, swims, crawls, strips. Somebody even had a sponsored wedding.

The women of the mining communities took on the task of turning the money into food and getting it through to those who needed it. Some groups set up food kitchens and cooked regularly, hot meals for hundreds of people. Other groups bulk-bought essential foods and distributed them in a weekly food parcel to miners in their area. The reasons why a group would do one or the other where largely a matter of chance – geography, transport, the existence of a convenient church hall and a friendly vicar could make all the difference.

There were advantages and disadvantages to both. Some people felt the kitchens would be too like the 'soup kitchens' of the '30s, with their dreadful stigma of poverty; and they thought people would be too proud to use them, and would prefer to prepare their own food at home. Also, a food parcel service was less demanding in terms of time, and left people free for other activities. However, the kitchens had the added advantage of acting as a focus for the community, and providing warmth, comradeship and information as well as food. But they were very hard work – often catering for hundreds with facilities more primitive than those of an ordinary domestic kitchen – and they left the women exhausted.

Dot Whitworth, a miner's wife, worked at the Kellingley kitchen,

one of the largest in Yorkshire producing around 400 meals a day, and she describes the punishing daily routine:

'The women work the kitchen in two shifts. I come down with the other girls for the morning shift, at about 7.20 am. Then the pickets start coming in for their breakfasts – we give them a fry-up with eggs, or sausages, beans or tomato, depending on what we've got.

When they've gone, we get cleaned up, and about 9 am I go down to the shops for bread and milk. The others start preparing the veg for the dinners.

About 11 am the lads come in to get their flasks filled up and have a hot drink before they go on local pickets.

Soon after that, people start coming in for their dinners – families with kids as well as pickets. We never turn anybody away. It's all a mad rush until about 1.30. Then the women sit down and have their lunches before they go off, and the afternoon shift arrives.

The six women on the afternoon shift come in about 1 o'clock. They help with the clearing up, and start preparing for teas.

The children often come in straight from school – sometimes they meet their parents down here – and we give them potatoes, fish or meat burger – something like that. We only have one large cooker so we can't go in for anything elaborate. In fact the kitchen is just a portakabin tacked onto the back of the club hall. We try to do meals that are cheap but nourishing – we don't have the cash or the kitchen-staff to do puddings for example.

From about 5 pm the pickets come in if we are still serving they'll have a dinner, and they'll have a hot drink and get their flasks filled. At 6.30 the women go home, and then the men take over. They wash up and clean and mop the tables, floor and stairs. It's quiet then until about 11 pm when the night pickets come in, and round about 12 the evening pickets come back.

As you can see, it's very hard work, but I must say, we do get a lot of help from the men. They help with the cleaning and washing up, with preparing the veg, and with all the carrying. My husband's always been quite good around the house, but there are other men who've done things in this strike they'd never done before. I don't know if they'll carry on after the strike, though. One of the men always says, "If I see another sausage after this strike's over, I shall throw it at my wife."

I work on the tea counter, and that's nice because I get to talk to all the lads when they come in. They laugh and joke, and it's wonderful to see their morale so high. They really make us feel they appreciate what we're doing, and that makes it all worth while. I'd do it over again.'

It is impossible to generalise about the miners' support groups – each one was unique. There were groups like the one at Kellingley, serving 400 meals a day, and there were tiny groups of two or three women giving out a weekly food parcel in little remote villages. In South Wales, the groups organised down a valley, bringing together all the pits and villages in that valley in a co-operative effort. Here, as in other parts of the country, the union men were strongly involved in the local support work. But in other places where pits had closed and men had been transferred people were travelling long distances to picket and there was therefore no link between a single pit union branch and the local community.

The women of the village thus had to organise independently of the union on behalf of all the miners in the villages wherever they worked. The village of Upton in Yorkshire was a typical example of this. It was called the 'village with thirteen pits' because after the local pit was closed the miners were transferred to no fewer than thirteen other Yorkshire pits. Their food kitchen, organised by the women in the welfare club, once more brought together the men who had been separated from each other after their pit had closed.

The support groups also played a very important role in the villages of the new Selby coalfield, bringing people together and creating a sense of community in an area where few of the mining families had been settled for long enough to feel at home. The fact that all Women Against Pit Closures groups were able to develop according to the local needs of their area was one of the great strengths of the movement. This was helped by the fact that it soon became clear that all the groups also had a lot of common experiences, and much they could share.

Coming together

The first time all the groups came together was at the Barnsley rally on May 12th 1984, and for those who were there it is still remembered as one of the high points of the strike. Some 10,000 women marched through Barnsley on a crisp, sunny day, to congregate at the Civic Hall. Sheila Capstick and Jean Blackburn, two miners' wives wrote:

'Crowds lined the street corners, people waving and applauding. Behind our group the women from South Wales kept bursting into song, making some of us feel alternately elated and tearful – familiar tunes sung in unfamiliar language but recognisable as songs of working people.

As we filed up the stairs into the Civic Hall all you could see were thousands of heads and above them banners waving from side to side. The colours were magnificent. Many of the T-shirts carried slogans which mentioned specific pits. It was as if the women were saying 'this is the pit I'm from and I'm proud of it'.

As people started to file onto the platform the hall filled with women chanting 'We will win, we will win, we will win'.

Each speaker had to wait for the audience to recover and the women's voices rang round and round the hall. It is not often that the National President of the NUM is unable to make himself heard – but Arthur Scargill had to wait a full ten minutes before the crescendo of singing and chanting began to subside. As he was speaking spontaneous singing broke out from the floor a few time and he had to pause and wait . . .

At about three thirty the rally ended and I made my way back to the car. There was a lot to remember. I knew that I had seen something remarkable and it had given me more strength than I knew I had. Things would never be the same again.'

In July, the NUM allowed the women from the Barnsley Women Against Pit Closures group to use a room at the NUM's Sheffield headquarters to answer queries and develop national and international contacts. On 22nd July the first National Conference of Women Against Pit Closures was held at Northern College, near Barnsley. Women came to the conference from each coalfield area, to hammer out a programme for the future.

The conference drew up plans for a national WAPC rally in London in August, and for a petition from the women of the mining communities to be handed in to the Queen at Buckingham Palace.

On August 11th, some 20,000 women and children descended on London in fleets of coaches plastered with posters and stickers. It was an exciting occasion especially for the women who had never been to London before, but also a very tiring one, as the march turned out to be much longer than expected. We marched through the centre of London past Downing Street – where everybody walked in silence and some scattered black flowers in the road – and the House of Commons, down to the Elephant and Castle where a giant 'cheque' was presented at the DHSS office, then on to a rally at Burgess Park, Camberwell.

Just as successful in their own way were the many local marches and rallies that took place in the coalfield areas, and the women's support groups were always there, with their own home-made banners and their collecting tins.

The national conference

On November 10th and 11th, a special delegate conference met at Chesterfield to draw up the aims of the National Women Against Pit Closures:

1) to ensure victory to the NUM in their present struggle to prevent pit closures and protect mining communities for the future;
2) to further strengthen the organisation of women's groups which has been built up during the 1984 miners' strike;
3) to establish a national women's organisation in all areas;
4) to develop a relationship between the NUM and the women's organisation at all levels;
5) to campaign on issues that affect mining communities, particularly peace, jobs, health and education;
6) to promote working class education for women;
7) to publicise all the activities of the National Women's Organisation at all levels.

Winter approaches

With autumn came the first scabs in several areas which had been solid up to then, and pickets started to concentrate on their own pits, while also keeping up a presence in Notts. Women in Notts and the Derbyshire and Yorkshire areas closest to the Notts coalfield already had considerable experience of picketing. But for the majority of women, their first experience was of standing on picket lines outside their own local pit, and shouting at men who had been receiving food from them only a week ago. It was a bitter experience. With the strike breakers came their police escorts, thousands of them, bringing fear and violence in their wake.

Winter came early in 1984. By November it was already bitterly cold, and while people welcomed the cold dark nights for the pressure they put on the coal stocks, it was no fun going back to a freezing house, especially if you didn't even have 50p for the electricity meter. Summer clothes were outworn, and there was no money for new ones. All the pickets had holes in their shoes. Children's clothes and shoes were a particular problem, for, in spite of everything, the children had carried on growing! Whereas in the past, jumble had been collected and sold to buy food, now it was laid out for people to help themselves, and men's shoes were always the first to go. The jumble which was shipped in from overseas was especially prized, being of a very high quality — in fact there are still many fancy coats and boots being worn around the coalfields which their owners will tell you, with a smile, came from supporters in West Germany.

The Labour-controlled councils in the coalfield areas deserve a special word of praise for their discreet and often unrecognised help to the strikers and their families. Rules were stretched to the limit and sometimes were broken to provide free school meals during holidays as well as school days, 'Section One' help to families with children, clothing grants, and even Christmas toys. It made a great difference, as those unfortunate to live in Tory-controlled areas found to their cost. An example of this can be seen by the fact that one little girl was sent home from school by her headmaster because she did not have a regulation pair of brown shoes — despite the fact that all her mother could afford was plastic jelly-bean shoes, and they didn't make them in brown. Her local council said it was not their policy to give grants for school clothes, and suggested she tell her husband to go back to work. The little girl had to stay off school until a pair of brown shoes the right size turned up in a bag of jumble.

As Christmas approached, with no sign of an end to the dispute, people began to feel nervous, especially about how they would explain to the children that they would not be getting so much that year. A special word of praise is due to the children of the mining communities — they went without such a lot, and complained so little. In the event, we need not have worried. Lorry loads of toys started to arrive, from France, Belgium, Germany, Holland, and from support groups all over Britain.

More important than toys and parties, though, were the warmth and togetherness of the community at Christmas.

The miners' support groups, who had already done a magnificent job of financial and moral support all through the strike, really went to town at Christmas. As well as toys and seasonal foods, they were able to provide for Christmas parties in most communites. The national Women Against Pit Closures appeal brought in almost £½ million and other individuals and unions made outstandingly generous donations. In fact many of the miners' families involved will say without hesititation: "We had the best Christmas of our lives".

After Christmas, with the weather still cold, many women spent more and more time alongside their menfolk on picket lines, trying to stem the steady flow of miners who were giving up the fight and returning to work. It was not a very happy time for them but the women played an important role in keeping morale up, with their singing and chanting, and organising social events.

With many miners' families now having no source of heating at home, the kitchens became more than ever a place where people came not just for a meal but to get warm, and to escape isolation. Inevitably in those close communities, many of the scabs were neighbours, relatives or former friends, and added to the general material hardship which people suffered was the hardship of losing people to whom one had been close, and who could never be close again.

As history now records, on March 5th the miners who had stayed loyal to the NUM marched back to work behind their banners. With them were the women who had sustained them through the strike. Heads were held high, but many had tears in their eyes. As one miners's wife said: "I feel as through someone close to me has died."

After the strike

However, underlying all the sadness was a new confidence on the part of the coalfield women. They saw so much still to do. They realised the knowledge, experience and strength gained through the strike hadto be consolidated and carried forward.

First of all, the miners who had been victimized as a result of their activities during the strike had to be looked after. Many women's support groups carried on fund-raising and campaigning on behalf of sacked and jailed miners and their families. In Scotland, for example, over 200 men had been sacked, and the Coal Board managers refused even to listen to any appeals.

Despite the setback of the NUM's June '85 decision not to offer miners' wives Associate Membership of the NUM, the union in Scotland has recognised this role in the strike and agreed to recognise women locally into Associate Membership, and women in other areas are hoping that their local NUM officials will follow suit. It must be said, however, that there are mixed feelings among the women on the question of Associate Membership; this is very much a reflection of the relationship built up between the women and their local NUM during the strike, as well as wider questions about the direction Women Against Pit Closures should take.

The future

There can be no question, however, about the women's continuing commitment to defending their pits and their communities. When the EEC Energy Commission drew up plans to remove coal subsidies and increase coal imports, the women responded with a petition. When the NCB launched its divisive campaign in Notts and South Derbyshire, the women organised meetings and leaflets, and stood outside collieries to sign up men for the NUM. When the Coal Board announces pit closures, women in those communities are at the heart of the new closure campaign groups which are springing up all over the country.

Women are also finding more time to explore other political avenues. The strike brought home to many of them for the first time how much they have in common with other people fighting for peace and justice, both at home and abroad. Miners' wives have visited Greenham Common and other peace camps, have stood on picket lines with hospital workers, have helped wives of strikers at the Silentnight factories who organised food kitchens, have contacted women in South Africa, Chile, Nicaragua and El Salvador.

Hucknall/Linby striking miners' kitchen. Brenda Prince/Format

Many women and children from mining communities have travelled overseas as guests of workers' organisations in other countries, and these links are still maintained. There has also been more time for reflection and developing some of the new ideas culled from the experiences of the past year. Women have started to write — histories, stories, poetry — and to join education classes and read and discuss, to argue more confidently, and to get involved in party politics.

Nationally, Women Against Pit Closures now has a delegate structure with a National Committee that meets monthly. It is based at the NUM headquarters in Sheffield, and has a regular newsletter, 'Coalfield Women'. They held their first national conference in August, and are planning a delegate conference for the spring.

Further, in their own towns and villages, women who were active during the strike are putting their campaigning and organising skill to good use for the benefit of the whole community. Women have joined fights against hospital closures, and for better local medical facilities. They have fund-raised for local charities, and for other groups in need.

In Llanhillieth, Gwent, the women's support group is now campaigning for a new Community Centre, which will incorporate a day-centre, training workshops to help create new jobs in the area, and, last but not least, a creche. In Castleford, Yorks, women are in the process of setting up a Women's Centre with the help of a County Council grant. In the North East, women's support groups are linking up with peace groups and environmental groups to fight pit closures — and their replacement with a nuclear power plant. In Sherburn, North Yorks, women leafleted and campaigned during the local elections, and managed to win a previously safe Tory seat for Labour. These are just a few examples of the new directions the women's movement is taking.

Not all the women who were active during the strike are still involved. Hardship and demoralisation have taken their toll. Some families have had to sell their homes, and those women who have been able to find jobs are working to pay off massive debts. Many marriages have been through a rough patch, and the relentless pressure by management on men in the collieries affects the whole family. But as people get their finances straightened out the old fighting spirit is returning. For hundreds of women, the strike has opened new doors, and there will be no going back.

This song which the women of the coalfields have adopted as their

* Quotations have been taken from Barnsley Women Against Pit Closures, Vols I and II; Strike '84-'85 by North Yorkshire Women Against Pit Closures and Coalfield Women. The song Women of the Working Class, written by Mal Finch is performed by the group Flamin' Nerve and is available with other songs on tape from the WAPC office, c/o NUM, or on the Heroes album.

own, and which is heard at marches, rallies, and concerts up and
down the country says it all:

> We are women, We are strong,
> We are fighting for our lives
> Side by side with our men
> Who work the nation's mines,
> United by the struggle,
> United by the past,
> And it's — Here we go! Here we go!
> For the women of the working class.

8 Since the strike: pit closures

SINCE the pit strike ended in March 1985 the National Coal
Board has relentlessly cut back the industry.

17 pits were closed before the end of 1985 and 13 more proposed for
closure. The NCB says that since the end of the strike 19,500 men
have left the industry, including 15,500 opting for voluntary
redundancy. It says there has been a net loss of 17,500 men from the
industry because it has taken on 2,000 new recruits. There are still
593 miners dismissed after the strike and the National Union of
Mineworkers nationally renewed its offensive to win back the jobs of
the victimised men at a recent special delegate conference. On top of
this, long term plans have been put forward to cut the industry down
even more savagely than miners' leaders had predicted.

The new strategy for coal — which declares that there is no long
term future for pits at which coal costs £39 a tonne — leaves the
industry entirely at the mercy of the market. This free market
approach is diametrically opposed to Labour's plans for a planned,
coherent energy policy in a new plan for coal.

Miners' leaders predict that could mean 50 more pit closures and
50,000 jobs. Pit deputies' leaders are even more pessimistic and fear
that on the basis of pits having to have a 500,000 tonne capacity a
week and a two million tonne capacity a year then there would only
be 47 "superpits" left in the country. The NCB also announced that
in future pits would have to carry their own interest charges —
pushing pits otherwise considered 'profitable' into the danger zone.

Miners who were demoralised after the strike were panicked into taking redundancies and voting for pit closures because of the widely spread threat of loss of redundancy-linked benefits. The threat had a devastating effect in south Wales, in particular, where at one stage three pits in a week were forced to accept closure Celynen North, Abertillery and Penrhiwceiber.

Because of non-payment of national insurance contributions during the year-long strike, miners feared that if they failed to agree closure before the end of the year, they faced a possible loss of redundancy linked payments. To make things harder for the unions the coal board dragged its feet for a whole year on the agreement it had reached with the pit deputies Nacods over the new modified colliery review procedure.

The agreement described as 'sacrosanct' by government and the NCB was delayed as long as possible by the NCB to allow it to bring forward the maximum number of pit closures. The industry has been told it has got to 'break-even' in two years and be self-financing by the end of the decade.

The NUM fears that privatisation is at the end of this strategy and the Centre for Policy Studies is pressing its ideas of privatisation. Ian MacGregor's links with South African mining companies in the new Institute for Coal Development have led to fears about more coal coming in from South Africa as pits close in Britain. The 'free market' strategy for coal would fit into the jigsaw of privatisation plans.

The breakaway from the NUM has been given great support by the NCB which wants to move to dividing the industry into autonomous areas, with separate pay bargaining.

Miners leader's in Kent point to the fact that Snowdown colliery, which was one of the five pits at the heart of the year-long miners' strike, now earmarked for development of a new seven foot thick seam. This proves what is said by miners is true that there is no such thing as an uneconomic pit — just a pit without investment.

The 17 pits which have closed so far in 1985 are:

Acton Hall (N. Yorks)	July 5
Savile (N. Yorks)	August 23
Moorgreen (S. Notts)	July 19
Pye Hill (S. Notts)	August 9
Bedwas (S. Wales)	August 31
Celynen South (S. Wales)	September 6
Markham (S. Wales)	September 20
Treforgan (S. Wales)	September 30
Penrhiwceiber (S. Wales)	October 8
Abertillery (S. Wales)	October 9

Aberpergwm (S. Wales)	October 7
Wolstanton (Western)	October 18
Yorkshire Main (S. Yorks)	October 11
Brookhouse (S. Yorks)	October 25
Cortonwood (S. Yorks)	October 25
Brenkley (N. East)	October 25
St Johns (S. Wales)	November

The 13 proposed closures are all at various stages. Three closures have been agreed locally. They are: Glasshoughton, North Yorks, to close 1986; Whitwick, south midlands, close July 1986; Sacriston, North East, close December 1985. Polkemmet in Scotland is subject to national appeal requested by NUM and Nacods.

National appeals have been requested for Darfield Main, Barnsley, and held for Tilmanstone, Kent, andthe decision is awaited. Bates, and Hordern in the north east, have been referred to the independent review body finally set up only this month.

The proposed reorganisation of the Hawthorne combine mine (north east area) involving the elimination of surface facilities at Eppleton, Hawthorne, Murton combine — is also to be referred to the independent review body.

Other proposed closures on which appeals are yet to be decided are: Betteshanger, Kent, Emley Moor, Barnsley; Bold, western; Kinsley Drift, north Yorkshire, and Fryston, north Yorks.

The struggle continues

There is no doubt that the miners, during their heroic resistance of 1984-85, demonstrated that there *is* an alternative to meekly accepting the effects of this Tory government. But that struggle continues, not just for miners but for all working people and their families.

The miners have not been alone either in or during their strike and actions. Other unions and other groups of workers such as the NGA in their battle to retain trade unionism in Warrington and the resulting court action against them, the TGWU have faced up to fines and found the Queen's Remembrancer surfacing from the depths of history to steal their funds. Silent Night workers, Barking Hospital workers, Sheffield Forge workers and many others have been prepared to show courage and determination against this government and its policies.

But the miners' strike, more than others, stimulated a ground-swell of activity from fellow workers from every corner of this country to support their just struggle. The women of the pit villages combined with the people of suburban London, the rail workers in the Midlands and the nurses in the welsh valleys joined forces to assist their comrades in struggle.

This is the time for working people to stand together and build up a co-ordinated resistance whether against cut-backs in public sector services, attacks on the local body politic and local government, job losses and higher unemployment. The capitalist system is ferociously hanging on to its wealth as it prepares inevitably to make way for a fair and caring society where power is transferred to working people. The tories have shown their willingness to use the police and the judiciary and we must not shirk from those lessons when framing our legislation for the next Labour government.

The struggle of the NUM is not over, but neither is the struggle to get a Labour government elected that will relentlessly pursue socialist policies of peace, justice and freedom. When next a group of workers call on the Labour and Trade Union movement for help, let us be there to support them and continue the struggle which the miners have started.

What the miners have started, let the movement continue — a campaign for justice and for a just society.

 # Why Justice?

THE **Justice for Mineworkers** Bill has been introduced into the House of Commons, by the Campaign Group of Labour MPs, to give effect to composite resolution 69 which was carried by 3,542,000 votes in favour, with 2,912,000 votes against, at the Labour Party Conference in Bournemouth in October 1985.

This composite resolution concentrated on three issues: a review of cases, re-instatement and re-imbursement, and these are the points which have been incorporated into the new bill. A similar resolution had been passed by the Trades Union Congress at its meeting a month earlier and therefore this new bill can be said to have the support of a majority of both the industrial and political wings of the movement.

Although the Bill has been printed by the House it obviously has no prospect of being passed by the present parliament which has a massive tory majority in both the Lords and the Commons, and it is most unlikely that there will even be any time found to debate it.

But the real reason why the bill has been drafted and presented to the House of Commons is so that it could form a part of the nationwide political campaign in support of the miners, to which the conference also committed the party and copies of the **Justice for Mineworkers Bill** will be made available throughout the country.

This is, in fact, the third bill dealing with these questions that the Campaign Group of Labour MPs have submitted.

The first one called the **Democratic Amnesty and Unfair Penalities Repayment Bill** was introduced in 1982 and that very year the Labour conference endorsed its provisions.

The second one called **The Miners Amnesty (General Pardon) Bill** was presented to the House in the last session and was widely circulated around the movement.

The reason why this latest bill was drafted slightly differently is that the Campaign Group thought it right that we should follow the precise wording of the composite, so as to be absolutely in line with the decisions actually taken up the Labour Party Conference and the TUC Congress in 1985.

As members of the Labour Party will be aware the resolution concerning this matter was criticised at conference on the grounds that it constituted retrospective legislation, which is supposed to be contrary to the practices of British law. But this objection to retrospective legislation only applies if an act which is legal at the time it was taken, is made illegal at a later date, so that a person can be punished for something that was lawful when it was done.

There is absolutely no parallel if a full pardon is given later, for

acts which were held to be illegal at the time that they were performed, and amnesties have been given regularly in such cases. For example an amnesty was granted to Ian Smith and his illegal Rhodesian government in respect of everything that they did when they were in rebellion against the crown.

Similar amnesties have, for example, been given to all those who served in the armed forces and retained weapons that they should have handed in to the authorities when they were demobilised. After the end of almost every conflict it has been normal practice for general amnesties to be given to those who were involved, and when, for example, Britain withdraws from Northern Ireland — as she certainly will — there will be an amnesty for all those now serving sentences for acts of violence. No-one should therefore be influenced by that argument about retrospection, since it has no basis in past practice.

What is at stake is whether we, as the Labour movement, are able to insist that the next Labour government looks after our people in the same way that this government looks after its people.

But if we are to succeed we must build up our campaign now and win public support for it between now and the next general election, so as to get the pledge into Labour's manifesto, and get this Bill on to the statute book as soon as Labour has a majority in the House of Commons.

Tony Benn MP

Justice for Mineworkers Bill

A
BILL
TO:

Provide for a review of all cases of miners jailed as a result of the 1984-85 dispute in the mining industry; for the reinstatement of miners sacked for activities arising out of the dispute; for the reimbursement of monies confiscated as a result of fines, sequestration and receivership; and for purposes connected therewith.

Whereas during the heroic struggle of all who have been associated with the Miners Strike 1984-85, the National Union of Mineworkers and its membership have been the subject of a concerted and vicious attack by the whole power of the State, including the unprecedented and combined power of the police and the organised use of the judiciary by whom an order of sequestration was imposed and the elected trustees of the union were removed and replaced by a receiver appointed to run the affairs of an independent trade union; and

Whereas a great injustice was inflicted upon the Natonal Union of Mineworkers and its members and the members of other unions who assisted in the campaign to defend pits, jobs and mining communities; and

Whereas it is right and proper for these injustices to be rectified and remedied by the State through the enactment of legislation for that purpose:

Be it therefore enacted by the Queen's Most Excellent Majesty, by and with the advice and consent of the Lords Spiritual and Temporal, and the Commons, in the present Parliament assembled, and by the authority of the same as follows:

1) Her Majesty's Secretary of State for the Home Department shall immediately review the cases of all

miners jailed as a result of the 1984-85 mining dispute, and of all those who took part in the dispute and were punished for acts done in good faith for the purpose of safeguarding jobs, living standards, services or civil liberties, and following such review the Secretary of State shall grant free pardons wherever appropriate.

2) All persons to whom this Act applies shall be required to be offered re-instatement by the National Coal Board or other employer at their place of work, or at an alternative and suitable place of work without any loss of service or benefit.

3) Those who on grounds of retirement, health or other reasons are not able or willing to accept re-instatement shall be fully compensated for the financial losses that they have suffered as a result of their dismissal.

4) The National Union of Mineworkers and all other unions which were associated with them in the said dispute shall be re-imbursed by the Treasury for all those sums confiscated from them as a result of fines or otherwise expended whether by the union or in their name as a result of their sequestration and arising out of the appointment of a Receiver.

5) Any expenses of a Minister of the Crown incurred in consequence of the provisions of this Act, including any increase attributable to those provisions in sums payable under any other Act shall be defrayed out of money provided by Parliament.

6) This Act shall come into force upon the date which the Royal Assent is given.

7) This Act may be cited as the Justice for Mineworkers Act 1986.

What you can do

National Justice for Mineworkers Campaign

The National Campaign for Justice was launched to organise support for the NUM's campaign in defence of victimised miners. It was established from a meeting at the Labour Party Conference in Bournemouth organised jointly by the Campaign Group of Labour MPs, Trade Union Briefing, as well as a large number of NUM Area Defence Campaigns and Miners Support Groups.

The basis of its campaign is:

1) Support for the NUM resolutions to the TUC and Labour Party Conferences 1985.

2) To raise support for the sacked, victimised and imprisoned miners and their families and to raise money for the NUM National Solidarity fund.

3) To publicise the Justice for Mineworkers Bill and to campaign for its enactment by the next Labour government.

WHAT YOU CAN DO

● Join the Campaign. Rates: £50 National Organisations; £25 District Organisations; £5 Local organisations.
● Organise local meetings.
● Pass resolutions of support and send them to appropriate Trades Unions, Trades Councils, TUC, Labour Party, Home Secretary, individual MPs.
● Write to all MPs asking them to visit jailed miners.
● Visit the families and offer support to families of jailed miners.
● Write to prison governors about individual prisoners.
● Campaign in your Trade Union, Trades Council and Labour Party for the next Labour government to grant a general review of all cases, reinstatement and compensation to all miners sacked because of their activities in the dispute.

Cheques should be made payable to:
National Justice for Minerworkers Campaign, C/o Durham Mechanics Offices, Group no. 1 Area, 26 The Avenue, Durham DH1 4ED.

Coalfield Woman

The national newsletter of Women Against Pit Closures has news, views and plenty of action from around the coalfields.

If you would like to receive a copy regularly, please send a donation (£2.10 minimum for six issues) to:

> **WOMEN AGAINST PIT CLOSURES**
> **C/O NUM, ST. JAMES' HOUSE,**
> **VICAR LANE, SHEFFIELD**

If you would like to know more about Women Against Pit Closures write to the same address, giving your name, address, telephone number, the name of your support group (if any) and stating whether or not you are related to an NUM member.

PS If your support group is still active, why not write and let us know what you are doing.

Miners Solidarity Fund

In the wake of the twelve month NUM industrial dispute with the NCB, some 966 miners were sacked by the Coal Board. Despite all reasonable arguments by the NUM and representations by members of the House of Commons, they still refuse to reinstate at least 550 of them. Most have been dismissed for trivial or non offences and the majority were union branch officials whose crime was to fight for jobs and mining communities. At the time of writing this appeal 17 miners languish in jail on charges arising directly from the dispute.

The NUM is pledged to assist all its members to provide support for their families and to seek their reinstatement. The Miners Solidarity Fund is the only authorised body to work with the Union in providing financial support and only by all donations being sent directly to the fund can a fair distribution of resources be ensured.

We therefore urge the following actions:

- urge all members to fill in the banker's order form (below) to ensure regular monies to the fund;
- get your organisation to make a donation to the fund;
- organise benefit functions and support meetings;
- urge local authorities to continue to give support for all families affected;
- write to local and national newspapers, trades union journals and other media outlets in support of those affected.

Send all monies to: **Miners Solidarity Fund, St. James House, Vicar Lane, Sheffield**. Cheques and postal orders made payable to Miners Solidarity Fund or pay cash immediately through any bank quoting Miners Solidarity Fund, Co-op Bank, West Street, Sheffield Branch Account No. 300000009. Bank Sorting Code 08-90-75.

STANDING ORDER   Date: ....

Name of Bank _____

Branch _____

Name _____

Account No.   Signed: ....

I/We authorise you until further notice in writing to debit my/our account as above with the sum of £...
per week/month to commence on the ....
(date) and continuing each following week/month and to credit such amounts to the **Miners Solidarity Fund** account at the **Co-operative Bank PLC, West Street, Sheffield**.

Women Against Pit Closures

Head Office
K. Young
James Hse
Vicar Lane
Sheffield
South Yorks

Barnsley
L. Bowler
14 Dovedale Pl
Barnsley
South Yorks

Doncaster
B. Frante
Glenroyd
Doncaster Rd
South Elmsall
South Yorks

N. Yorkshire
M. Handforth
11 Waterearth
Kellington
Nr. Goole
Humberside

S. Yorkshire
P. Smith
7 Doequarry Terrace
Dinnington
Sheffield
South Yorks

Warwickshire
K. Hobson
2 Pembroke Cl
Bedworth
Nuneaton
Warwickshire

Staffordshire
B. Proctor
153 Broadway
Meir
Stoke on Trent
Staffs

Durham
A. Suddick
c/o Durham Mechanics
26, The Avenue
Durham City
Co. Durham

Kent
M. Holmes
234 Dover Rd
Deal
Kent

Leicester
K. Smith
35 Manor Rd
Barlestone
Nuneaton
Warwickshire

Northumberland
A. Lilburn
15 Hedgehope Cr
Hadstone
Morpeth
Northumberland

South Wales
K. Jones
7 Lincoln Cl
Tennysylvannia,
Llanedeyrn
Cardiff
South Wales

North Wales
L. Cheetham
26 Warren Dr
Prestatyn
North Wales

Scotland
E. Eagan
c/o 5 Hillside Crescent
Edinburgh
Scotland

Lancashire
S. Pye
34 Maple Ave
Newton-Le-Willows
Merseyside
Lancs

Derbyshire
L. Dennett
54 Birch St
Church Warsop
Mansfield
Notts

Notts
P. Oldfield
25 Beckett Ave
Mansfield
Notts

Miners Support Groups

National Justice
For Mineworkers
Campaign,
49 Milner Sq.
London N1.

Northumberland &
Durham MSG
26 The Avenue
Durham DH1 4ED
(A. Suddick)

Rhymney Valley MSG
218 Paudy Rd
Bedwas Gwent
(Ray Davies)

Medway MSG
283 Barnsole Rd
Gillingham Kent
(S. Hancock)

Oxford Trades Council
MSG
63 Bartlemas Rd
Oxford
(Alan Thornett)

South Yorks Defence
Campaign
Flat 2, 1 Agden Rd
Sheffield 7
(Flis Callow)

Lewisham MSG
34 Tresillian Rd
London SE4
(Nick Howitt)

Bridgwater MSG
4 Gordon Terrace
Bridgwater Somerset
(Glen Burrows)

Leeds District LP MSG
9 Queen St
Leeds 2
(John Appleyard)

Barnsley Miners Wives
Action Group
20 Windhill Crescent
Douton, Barnsley
Yorks
(Betty Cook)

Leeds MSG
41 Hartley Crescent
Leeds
(Sue Hobbs)

Burnley MSG
184 Brunshaw Avenue
Burnley, Lancs
(Dave & Barbara
Passingham)

Bath MSG
48 Stirtingale Rd
Bath
(Mike Polley)

Richmond &
Twickenham MSG
28 The Green
Twickenham, Mddx
(Ed Affard)

South Yorks Sacked
Miners Association
10 Sorrel Rd
Sunnyside
Rotherham, Yorks
(Dave Boyle)

Birmingham Trades
Council MSG
7 Frederick Street
Birmingham B1 3HE

Swansea MSG
110 Fabian Way
Port Tennant, Swansea
West Glam SA1 8PA
(Brendan Young)

Hammersmith & Fulham
MSG
6 Doris Rd
London SW6
(Vernon King)

Islington MSG
49 Milner Square
London N1
(Shosh Morris)

Exeter MSG
91 Park Road
Exeter
(Neil Todd)

North West MDC
Moss Side Peoples Centre
Manchester M15 5WA
(Rick Summer)

Southampton MSG
c/o NUPE District Office
93 Leigh Road
Eastleigh, Hants
(Richard Jewison)

Leeds Miners Defence
Ctte
16 Newport Gardens
Leeds LS6 3DA
(Phil Coyne)

Coventry MSG
11 de Compton Close
Keresley, Coventry
(D Jones)

S th Yorks Sacked Miners
c/o 2 Redland Way
Maltby, Rotherham
Yorks

Darfield Community
Action Committee
17 Rimington Rd
Wombwell
Barnsley, S Yorks
(M Marshall)

Agecroft Strike Ctte
c/o AUEW Building
43 The Crescent
Salford
(Steve Howells)

Welbeck Amnesty Group
PO Box 1
Worsop, Notts
(Billy Seaton)

St Johns & Darfield
Joint Ctte
c/o 67 Ravensdale Rd
London N16

Lancaster MDC
4 The Group
Lancaster
(John King)

Leeds MDC
47 Hartley Crescent
Leeds LS6 2LL
(Frankie Blagden)

Southwark Trades Council
MSG
42 Braganza Street
London SE17
(Vince Brown)

Beckenham & Penge
Amnesty Campaign
79 Wadhurst Close
London SE20 8TA
(Joyce Earl)

Yorks Miners Campaign
Group
34 Corporation St
Barnsley, South Yorks
(Neil Parry)

Deeside MSG
21 Chichester St
Chester CH1 4AD

Coventry
37 Fullbrook Rd
Coventry CV2 1FN
(M Jones)

Collectif d'Information et
de Soutien aux Mineurs
Britainniques
14 rue de Nanteuil
75015 PARIS France

Chorley Support Group
32 Coppull Hall Lane
Coppull, Chorley,
Lancs
(Rita Aspinall)

Deeside MSG
Baines House
Glynne Street
Queensferry
Deeside, Clwyd

Barnet MSG
4 Corringway
London NW11 7ED
(Peter Grimes)

Harringey MSG
628-630 Green Lanes
London N8
(Jo & Fay)

Barking & Dagenham
MSG
14 Porters Avenue
Dagenham
Essex RM8 2AQ
(Ian Barber)

Brent MSG
70 Dewsbury Rd
London NW10
(Richard Lynch)

Camden MSG
Planning & Comm. Dept
Camden Town Hall
Extension
Argyle St
London WC1
(Dave Wylson)

City MSG
c/o Library
The Guardian
119 Farringdon Rd
London EC1
(John Rogers)

Ealing MSG
West London TU Club
30-33 Acton High St
London W3
(Jim Green)

Enfield MSG
17 Hawthorn Rd
Edmonton
London N18 1EX
(Dave Buxton)

Greenwich MSG
32 Woolwich Rd
London SE10

Hackney MSG
Hackney TUSU
489 Kingsland Rd
London E8
(Fred Cattle)

Hounslow MSG
37 Albion Rd
Hounslow, Middx
(Cecia Dighan)

Ilford & Redbridge MSG
Ilford Unemployed Ctre
203 Ilford Lane
Ilford, Essex
(Charlie Say)

Lambeth MSG
75 Stockwell Rd
London SW4
(Nick Phillips)

Neath & District MSG
63 Church Rd,
Seven Sisters
Neath
West Glam, Wales
(Christine Powell)

Waltham Forest MSG
23 Worford Rd
London E17
(Bob Tenant)

Stoke MSG
170 High Street
Alsager Bank
Stoke on Trent
Staffs
(Jill Ebury)

Denbeigh MSG
Tyddyn ISA Llannefydd
Nr Denbeigh
Clwyd, N. Wales

York MSG
26 Wentworth Rd
York YO2 1DG
(Danny Golding)

Yorks Miners Solidarity
57 Micklegate
York

Oldham Support Group
31 Bath St
Oldham, Lancs
(Paul Keleman)

Hampstead MSG
48 Goldhurst Terrace
London NW6 3HT
(Cathy Lowe)

York MSG
3 Scaife St
York
(Terry)

Birkenhead MSG
TV Resource Centre
Argyll St South
Birkenhead

Colchester MSG
Colchester Labour Club
West Chapel Street
Colchester Essex

Cardiff MSG
14 Rawden Place
Riverside
Cardiff
(Anne Ogle)

Hull MSG
33 Raglan Rd
Newland Avenue
Hull
(Ian Dolphin)

Preston MSG
TV Centre
St Mary's Street North
Preston, Lancs
(John Parkinson)

Leicester MSG
56 Stephens Road
Leicester

Bristol MSG
c/o Transport House
Victoria St
Bristol BS1

University College of
London MSG
Flat 12
44-46 Frognal
London NW3
(A. Burls)

Left Out
162 Elmhurst Mansions
Edgeley Rd
London SW4
(Bruce Francis)

Islington MSG
80 Westbourne Rd
London N7
(Maggi Morrison)

Merton MSG
Merton Resource Centre
240 Merton Rd, SW19 1FQ
(Masie Carter)

Southall MSG
50-52 King St
Southall, Middx
(Eve Turner)

Tower Hamlets MSG
59 Bow Rd
London E3
(Mike Gavin)

Westminster MSG
40 Tachbrook St
London SW1
(Derek)

Black Delegation to the
Mining Communities
152-156 Shaftesbury Ave
London WC2H 7ED
(Tay)

Printed and bound by CPI Group (UK) Ltd, Croydon, CR0 4YY

22/04/2026

02095406-0007